PANDEMIC CITY

CITY

Caitlin Grace McDonnell

If your life is burning well, poetry is just the ash.

—LEONARD COHEN

PANDEMIC CITY

Copyright © 2021, Caitlin Grace McDonnell. All rights reserved.

Published by Nauset Press

nausetpress.com

New York

Cover image: *Pandemic Painting 4* or *NYC Pandemic Skyline 4* Acrylic on Paper,
original is 7.5" x 9.5" completed April 2020 © 2020 Jessica Nissen
www.jessicanissen.com

ISBN: 978-0-9907154-8-1

Pandemic with Love appeared in Across the Social Distances on 4/1/20

Pandemic with Possibility of Death, *Pandemic with Grief and Lungs*, and *Pandemic with City and Endings* first
appeared on Global Pandemic (https://globalpoemic.wordpress.com/category/caitlin-
grace-mcdonnell/)

For New York City

CONTENTS

FOREWORD

Pandemic, writes Caitlin Grace McDonnell, "fills the world like a giant select and delete." It threatens to erase self after self, melting ill, dead, dying, and affected in the sickening forge of statistic, smelting us into hard numbers, each ugly-exquisite life flattened into the grim pomp ever-receding into our pixilated scrolls. Abetted by quarantine, which is itself a necessary erasure, pandemic annihilates us twice. The statistic is an iterative unremembering.

In this context of erasure, with this book in hand, there is no mistaking the humanity of the lyrical narrative. McDonnell's *Pandemic City* makes clear, the lyrical narrative is a curative. The emotional experience of the self in the body, writ in lived details of delight and suffering, of getting by, won't save us from Covid-19. Science must do that. But it does something as critical for our well-being. It inoculates us against erasure: "No longer can she wade through/the department emails but knows/she needs to make lists of students/who have disappeared. She asks/them to check in." And check in they do: One has an exhausting frontline job, another is stress baking; all are determined to finish school. Documenting their words, the poem witnesses to their humanity. It rescues each of them, in their uniqueness, from the list.

In the face of a pandemic (and in the bureaucracy of the pandemic), such a poetry is a resistive project. Along with the Indian poet VK Sreelesh, I curate the website

Global Poemic, gathering poems that witness to Covid-19. In a unique circumstance for a site that normally mounts a single poem a day, we published three poems by McDonnell, included herein: *Pandemic with Possibility of Death*, *Pandemic with City and Endings* and *Pandemic with Grief and Lungs*. In the titular syntax of still life paintings, McDonnell's titles announce the pandemic as a totalizing condition, the grey, flat ground of our shared canvas of lock down, death, and survival. But, against it, McDonnell's details pop. This is how the poet writes herself, and all of us, into existence, with painstaking precision. Taken as an entirety, this book—this litany of *Pandemic with*'s—is, for each of us who lives and each who has died, a manifesto: "Nobody can become/me after I am gone."

—BETSY ANDREWS, *Brooklyn, New York, January 16, 2021*

PANDEMIC WITH LOVE

Hungover from two Zoom cocktail hours in one night.

The rain says, *Let me make this easy for you.*

But I don't do easy, so will get wet.

My lover says, *We can't*, then *we can.*

Each hand is 100 hands.

The children grapple with the concept of fair.

The adults grapple with the concept of fair.

The person whose smoke comes in through the vents

smoked all night and then mercifully, not at all.

Or else I have become her smoke.

I love the woman in the elevator smiling

from the other end, saying her name twice

Saying we should check on the woman in 4E.

I love the Callen-Lorde nurse who prescribed

anti-anxiety pills, paused and said, *What about*

your migraines and how are you doing? And paused.

For a real answer. With no sense of having to go.

I love the woman on the other side of the building

who said I am easy to please in response to

my telling her I love her in response to

her Showtime password. It's showtime, folks.

Close the windows. Electric chatter.

Rich raspberry dark.

PANDEMIC WITH CORD

In what could have been the last time I saw my mother,
I tripped over a cord running between us.
She was watching *Call the Midwife*
on her cell phone on my couch as I dunked
my thin middle-aged girl body in a bath
of warm saltwater. *You're leaving me,*
she'd said. *I'm just taking a bath,* I sighed.
Vanessa Redgrave and a superfluity of nuns
shouting out tiny cell speakers from the couch
while the phone cord stretched low and tight
across my living room to charge. I was naked
in a white towel my lover who was leaving me
had given me, which fell to the floor
when I tripped, and my mother screamed,
You pulled my arm. Mother, daughter, cord.
My falling hurt her, pulled her dislocated
shoulder out, and in that dark, she couldn't see
me, naked on the floor. Love causes pain.
My own daughter's head resting on my
occipital ridge as she surrenders
to sleep is slowly carving a cave
of pain. My mom had that shoulder
replaced last week, as this virus
fills the world like a giant select
and delete. My sister's girlfriend,
a nurse, who cared for my mom
after the surgery, has a fever.

The kinds of decisions we make now,

not unlike the ones we make for birth,

packing bags, making playlists in vain.

What will happen will happen.

The world will go dark before the light.

At the end of it, there will be some green,

some breath,

a cord to cut.

PANDEMIC WITH TEFILLIN

She went to the lover's house.
Even though all day, the phone,
the road signs, blinking with alerts.
Stay Home. Stay Home.
On her bike, the streets seemed
oiled. People masked and unmasked
walked in slow motion.
In her earphones, PJ Harvey:
I'm in New York.
No need for words now.
They don't hug at first.
She washes her hands.
Are you feeling worried—
You can still change your mind.
She puts her body against her body.
Now I can't. The pandemic
creates monogamy before
they would have. *If she*
has to be called a mystery person,
says the daughter, *why*
is she in our germ circle?
At night, the lovers light candles,
and for a time it is just them.
They talk about times the light
penetrated the top of their skulls
alone in vast canyons. Times
of more truth than a body

can hold. They reach inside
one another and are bodies
and more than bodies.
Carrying or not carrying.
Fingers and flesh. Wet
with currents of desire.
But later, the others come in.
They let them in through cracks
with words and a small sea
parts between them. Hearts
wrap another layer, they hold
hands across the divide.
When she wakes at four,
which is when the new world
wakes her, she is grateful for
another body to brace against
the fear. She wakes again at seven
to find the mystery person standing
over the bed, wrapping her flesh,
freckled arms and chest,
in dark leather straps,
a little tighter than usual,
to be closer to God.

PANDEMIC WITH SCATTER

Now they are saying
the virus is killing younger people,
which fucks with the bargains
they made to control it.
Now capitalism is kicking
and screaming. Charcoal masks
with activated carbon on sale
on social media. The choice
between free yoga classes
and supporting the teachers
who used to touch her neck
when she still makes less money
than the teachers everyone is saying
deserve a raise. Her students
email asking for help, thanking her
and she closes her eyes and tries to see
their faces as she reads their words
about the story they read whose title
like everything, now seems laden
with metaphor: *Where Are You Going,
Where Have You Been?* The man from the
animal shelter who yelled at her about
the meaning of the word *foster*, when she
said, *I thought it meant it allowed us both
to change our minds*, was still yelling
about why doors were locked, what
it means to care for something alive.

She took her daughter and walked
away, and he became just another man
yelling, about something
he thought she needed to understand.
Meanwhile, at 4 am, the world
breathed, she breathed, like
a baby in an incubator
without a name.

PANDEMIC WITH PIPES

She wakes to the sound of water running.
It's the toilet. She pees, and it splashes her,
and she wonders if the virus
could be in the pipes and now
enter her through her cunt, mean-
while the neighbor texts on messenger
that her son has a fever and they
have no water at all to hydrate him.
Her super comes in the night
with tools, fixes the toilet,
Lotta problems tonight.
Lotta problems. She tries
to sleep but sees faces
changing to sick faces,
rooms without enough beds.
She sinks to a place where she's
always known this was coming.
Felt it deep in her bones.
It's what made following
the rules of the clock hard.
the rules of the clock,
and saying goodbye.

PANDEMIC WITH HAPPINESS

Today, they sit in the park.
Sun on the face, girls doing
handstands in the grass.
Not so close, she yells every once
in a while. They wonder aloud
how they'll recover from this,
given the chance to recover.
Now, when they watch TV,
it seems strange, all the touching
people do, jostling in hallways
hand on a casual hand,
cavalierly sharing food.
Are they not doing math
about how many touches hands
each hand is from death?
She lies in bed with her college
friends on little screens. One
is working more than ever
to absorb everyone's anxiety.
One is dating. Meeting new
men from six feet away on
mountain trails. *They all seem
the same*, she reports, *but it's
fantastic that we can't touch*.
On Facebook, someone reports
from a virtual dance party of
8,000 people, including FLOTUS

and Millie Bobby Brown.
At night, she is naked with
her lover across town, who
works hard to ground her in
release, *Our skin is touching,*
and I'm inside you, but tonight
she's found her singularity.
Turns off all the screens,
lights a candle with lemon
verbena labeled *Happiness*
from the last visit to the co-op,
stretches her limbs in the hot
water, which is finally back on,
adding some lavender salts, closes
her eyes, asks the world
to do what it will.

PANDEMIC WITH MAKEUP

It is a place now, what
spiritualists call being
shut off from God,
what psychiatrists call
despair, what *Stranger Things*
called the upside-down.
The place where she knew
this would happen, where she
sees too much truth
at once. The daughter
feels it in her. Connection
is a pond we stare into
trying to see beyond
our own reflection.
Let's give each other
makeovers, she suggests,
and together, they take down
all the dresses she will later need
to put back alone. Blue velvet,
red satin. They stuff tissues in
a leopard brassiere she bought
at a Santa Cruz yard sale, hold
still and close eyes for a line of
dark like a sentence in newsprint;
lips, red as the cinnamon candy
from the bin she used to reach into
with her bare hand. They fight

about the outfits, relinquishing
control. *Fine, make me however
you want,* she relents to a sweater,
french-tucked into an old skirt.
They stand against the wall and
take selfies to blast at the world
through the little screen, each
willing years to add or subtract
from their ages. To pose is to leave
the body, to transform it into
signage as we disappear,
as I did when my mom was lost,
driving home in the dark, cursing
at god knows what, no longer able
to pretend she knew
where we were.

PANDEMIC WITH LIMITS

They are starting to feel

the limits between them.

You can always come here,

she tells her friend

whose university apartment

will be made into a hospital

soon, *but long-term, I think*

you will want a bed. Her sister

cries on FaceTime, her divorcing

lover is back together with his

wife, doesn't respond at all

to her texts, as if they never happened.

I feel the truth of my lover's

limits, a woman on Instagram writes to her

and asks her for tea after the apocalypse.

It's a date, she responds. *We can do virtual*

if it doesn't end. All day, her phone

says her sign-in is blocked. *How*

is it there? She asks the Apple Support

guy in Oregon. *What is the name*

of your best friend in high school? Asks

the phone. *If it doesn't end,*

maybe gin, she writes the woman.

We're sandwiched between

two bad places, says Apple

Support. *What is the name of*

the street you grew up on? Asks

the phone. She runs in the rain
trying not to touch anything,
comes home, and takes off all
the wet clothes. Puts them in the pile
of things that have been outside.
The daughter is lunging with
weights with a woman in pink
on the TV for credit in gym,
giggles when she joins her,
naked, and corrects her form.
How could you not know I like Queen?
She asks, when they pick a tune.
If it's too far to bike, says her friend
the nurse, *you can drop it*
in the mail, regarding the box
of masks her quarantined
neighbor says will arrive
in their lobby. Student links
with *Invitation to Edit*
crowding her inbox.
She texts the sister a heart
emoji, texts the friend,
I'll drop it in the mail.

PANDEMIC WITH FRUIT

A day without a poem
because the morning was different—
not alone. Also, perhaps
too many people had read them.
Dickinson's tight words
are letters to the soul in part
because she kept them close, only
shared once or twice. *Open me,*
carefully, she wrote to her brother's
wife, whom she'd meet for brisk
and passionate walks before
she grew too ill to leave home.
Will this go in a poem, her lover asks
about the toasted rice tea, the floss
she hesitated to share, after they open
a crack in the quarantine, to find a vast
field where they are human. *No,*
once you say it, it can't. They grasp
at the body against the body to find
their own. Why does eye contact
during sex always remind us that
we have the power to take one
another's life? The hand holds
intention, to read, to build, to kill.
All that you touch, you change, said
Butler. We keep them gloved
now, trying to change as little

as we can, but when we reach inside
another, we touch the first wound, salty
wave, life's divine replenishment.
She (or I) had a hard time leaving, takes
a banana and some stamps to send
the masks to her (my) friend treating
bodies on the frontlines. She'd spared
description. Asked about daughters,
said, *If there's any way to get masks,*
that's what we need. The same friend
who said in a staff circle,
I want to shout out Caitlin,
for teaching me the strength
in being feminine. By the end
of the day, the banana is brown
on the outside, so I take it
out of its skin, put it in
the freezer with the others
I didn't get to eat in time.

PANDEMIC WITH MONEY

She buys the daughter a treat
wearing gloves and a mask, using
the $20 in her wallet, leaves the coins
but takes the bills, looks up how long
to wait before she can touch them again.
No longer can she wade through
the department emails but knows
she needs to make lists of students
who have disappeared. She asks
them all to check in. A says: *Hi,
Professor, so I'm doing fine but
I must say I am very tired. My job
is still open since I work at a supermarket
and I still go to work ... I can do this.
I'll just take it one day at a time.*
J: *My fridge is full of waffles, cheesecake,
brownies, and probably banana bread
by tomorrow if I'm feeling sad enough, lol.*
D: *I won't let this coronavirus
or anything stop me from completing
any of my courses.* Meanwhile, her
friend texts that Cape Elizabeth is
shutting down all short-term rentals
and hotels. *We are going to Camden
and crossing our fingers that the town
won't create a no-New Yorker policy,
too.* Meanwhile, she does laundry

in the basement with gloves, envies
the quarantined with machines
inside their apartments, but grateful
it's within the foundation of this
building, built in 1934, by immigrants,
who came here on boats, huddled
and rocking with hope in the sea air,
working outside day and night, with
beautifully calloused hands.

PANDEMIC WITH WATER

A day with abundant sun.
Can they all be outside?
You should go. It makes you
happy, says the daughter.
And who knows how long
the beach will be open, says
her father. *If they close the*
parks and beaches, I won't
be okay, she says before
realizing how ridiculous
this sounds. She drives
by herself with windows
that won't open (because
she can't find the right
mechanic or little plastic fuse)
out to Brighton
where people tend to walk
briskly and a little too close.
Her body says, *Stop*.
You can't run from it.
Sit down. She sits long
enough to feel the sun
warm her forehead, the edges
of her scalp, to hear the water,
let the rhythm of the waves
slow her breath inside
the epicenter of the epicenter

on this corner of this sand
where she is safe. Then she
strips down to her organic black
cotton underwear, which looks
enough like a swimsuit and
wades into the water, which
is salty and cold on her skin
so that the fine hairs stand up,
nipples and cunt hard with
attention, like a fist or a prayer.
A woman on the shore in a mask
is filming her, so she waves before
diving back in for seven strokes,
walks out as sun and salt mix
on her skin on her yellow towel
on this little spot of earth.

PANDEMIC WITH SIRENS

She orders food from the neighborhood
restaurant where she ran a reading series,
and they'd set up a mike for poetry and give
her free glasses of rosé with elderflower liquor;
she'd send them photos of poets in the corner light.
It's family, Jeremiah had said, handing her the new
baby while he checked the phones, *you're part
of the neighborhood family.* He asks if she wants
delivery or pick up, and the question lingers.
Is she risking someone else's life if she lets them
come to her; she looks at the daughter whose
skin looks computer grey and says, *You know what,
we'll come get it. You can't make me,* says
the daughter, and they both sit with the truth
of this, and the lie. They scoot with masks
and gloves over the overpass. *If you wanted
to help them,* the daughter says, *they'd have
made more money with the delivery fee.*
Just, please, be nice to me, she begs the smart-
ass daughter, *because I'm doing my best.*
Do you want a to-go cocktail? Asks Jeremiah
as he hands her the brown bags,
which she places on her handlebars.
He looks disappointed when she says
she is stocked, and she can't tell,
more than usual, what is love and
what is money. In the elevator,

she accuses the daughter of touching
her face with the same gloved hand
with which she touched the button.
Stop it, Mom, she says, *I didn't touch it.*
She sends the daughter inside as she plates
the food in the hallway. It's cold now,
the food, and it doesn't taste like it does
when inside the yellow glow of Della's
interior. She eats both her plate
of mushroom gnocchi and the daughter's;
lets her live on meatballs and buttered bread
and lemon dessert which tastes
like something raw. Is that still okay?
Was it ever? At night, after reading the
story about the owl home alone
who can't decide whether to go
upstairs or down, running up and
down until he collapses in the middle,
they turn out the light and do rose
and thorn. *The food wasn't as good*
as I thought it would be, says K.,
but we are almost done with Glee.
She falls asleep holding her,
as she's done for eleven
years, all her cells wrapped
around her as long as she
and the world will let them.
When she wakes in the night,
there are pills to take, a body
alone to soothe, as sirens

careen down the parkway out

her window in the rainy

night. (*I counted six between*

12 and 12:30 am, says the neighbor,

whose son was coughing blood.)

The food expanding in her belly

makes her sweat, almost feels

like sickness. *I am breathing fine,*

she tells her chest again, waits

for morning when the city

is so still, she can actually

hear a bird and no cars.

PANDEMIC WITH INVENTORY

Morning sirens wake her,
and six people send a story
about a choir gone deadly—
Sixty people singing without
touching, forty-five sick, two dead.
What this means is it hangs
in the air, writes the woman,
from her sick bed whose doctor
berated her for riding a bike.
She thinks of her deep inhales
in the wet air in the park
that made her pull her hoodie
up around her throat. Amazon
workers are walking out demanding
face masks, and GE workers are
walking out demanding to make
them. John Prine's in critical
condition, so everyone's playing
"Angel from Montgomery." *Just*
give me one thing that I can hold
onto. Some things have become
clear in quarantine. She doesn't
tolerate gluten anymore, or men.
She's in a quarantine-specific
love affair, needs a different
job and a different home. At night,
she dreams of faceless men taking over

screens, her father, a blue pool, Renae

with her sweet face, forgiveness, androgyny.

All the portals formerly closed. *In the rush*

to return to normal, a friend reminds

her, *maybe consider which parts*

of normal we want to hold on to.

PANDEMIC WITH CITY AND WEIGHT

In her weekly Zoom session
with the group they call *lil' chill,*
everyone is in attendance but Forest
Moon, out on a bike
in the San Fernando Valley.
The other New Yorker has COVID,
but he's drinking a beer. Says he
can't taste or smell it. Josh says
he won't get sex for three weeks
because he neglected to wear
gloves or a mask when he picked up
the folder about the prisoners
he's trying to get released. Carla
talks to them from bed, to distinguish
what they're doing from work.
Yesterday, fear took over.
If it stops your breathing and it's
in the air, then when can we breathe?
The government declared guns
essential items, and she'd bleached
the outside of an apple, forgetting
what's poison. On Twitter,
a New Yorker tries to sing out his
window like they did in Italy.
Shut the fuck up, yells his neighbor.
She remembers being stuck on
the Bay Bridge from San Francisco

for two hours as man was
counseled not to take his life.
If that was New York, Victor
had said, *it would have lasted
ten minutes. People woulda yelled
just fucking jump already.* After 9/11
her sister heard men at the corner
talking, *You bet,* they'd said.
*We're going to rebuild
those motherfucking towers.
We'll build three of 'em,* as
he flipped the bird, *shaped
just like this.* Today, she will try
to cover the sound
of the ambulances
with music, Ramit's NYC
marathon play list. *Chariots of Fire.*
Frank Sinatra,Lou Reed,
whom she met standing in line
for Leonard Cohen the year
before they both died. Cohen down
on his knees, bowler hat to heart.
Today, she interrupts her poem
to do an exercise routine with
the old PTA president, a former
Pontani Sister, who performed
burlesque on Letterman and
around the globe. *Heyyyy,
Caïtlin,* she beams from her
basement across Brooklyn.

Sweaty with generosity,

Go for the heavy weights,

today. Do what you can.

PANDEMIC WITH EDIBLES AND SLEEP

There are many things
these days that make her feel
like she wants to feel different
from how she feels. The rapist
usurper who won't go away, the
planet boiling as she tells her child
to do her online math, this pandemic
asking us to choose not to touch,
the stranger in the laundry room
who could cause harm. She suggests
to the lover that they eat an edible
because why not feel different.
White with a splash of red, she can't
recall if this one makes one sleep
or think. She splits it along the red
circle, and they each place it
in their mouths like the body
of Christ. Takes a long time to chew.
They don't feel it until she is on top
in indigo light and her lover scratching
an itch she didn't know was there.
The surrender reverberates, like a pebble
in a still lake, circles and circles out.
Hours later though, it still sits in her,
moving around her body
like a searchlight. Here is pain;
here is weight; here is want. Thoughts too;

there is a portal of worry, well,
now, that we're here. All night,
awareness shoots up the back
of her vagus nerve like a storm.
In the morning, forgiveness,
light. Coffee, a dip in cold
saltwater, which, later, she needs
to warm for her daughter
to gargle twice daily to keep
the infection in her tooth
from spreading. Take away capital,
and all doctors are witches.
This is what it feels like
inside the empire as it falls.
Today, the sun is giving us
a chance. Nicole's Mom is
negative. Yoli is negative.
She and the daughter take
screen breaks, scoot around
the block, just once. *I think
I'm done*, says Kaya, and
she doesn't push. Thorn,
I was tired today, Rose,
The sun was out. Bud,
We'll go outside again,
tomorrow.

PANDEMIC WITH EXES

The most recent one
she never really said
goodbye to. Or maybe
that was all they ever did.
She'd been to China. Jet lagged
in her living room, cried
on her couch, cried
in her bed, cried during
Jojo Rabbit at the Nitehawk,
where the waitress asked
who the beer was for, thinking
they were mother and child.
(Remember theaters? New ones
with food and drinks?) Who
can leave a child? She was
never consistent about
consequences. If you yell
like that in my house, she'd
threaten, I'll have to ask you
to leave. But what if she left?
They'd said goodbye
on the phone, just before
she saw her actual child
across the street, dropped
her ear pods down the air shaft.
Then she asked to join Christmas.
She'd fought with her mother,

needed a new family
for the day, brought ice wine tea
from the border and Jack Daniels
made in IPA barrels for them to swig
after dunks in cold water. They made
love and came together like always.
Soul to soul with loud cries
and photogenic ghosts.
Then she says, *I'm poly now,*
can't be primary, met a woman
on FaceTime in Saskatchewan.
There was a vibe. Then she says,
What do you mean you don't like
sandwiches. I've seen you eat
sandwiches. Then they said goodbye
on a trail with more yelling,
then in a car with a kiss on the neck.
Then she says, *Let's not talk*
until February, or maybe March.
Then, *let's meet, but not now,*
for a hike, when it's warm,
say hi to your kid.
She writes to ask if she's alive
and no answer. So she says,
If you don't answer, I'll have
to ask your parents. She says, *Hey,*
I'm okay. Hope you're alright,
it sounds nuts there. As the sirens
blare out in the night, each one
is a stranger she's seen

at a store, on the divider

between the streets of the parkway,

body to body on the rush

hour train. She takes a photo

of the sparkly coasters, scrub, mug,

three items that evoke her. She writes

the next day, *To be upfront, I'm*

seeing someone seriously, not

sharing the sentimentality

I'm receiving in those pictures.

Take care, it sounds bad

where you are. Bowl full of bees.

Back turned, covered in rash,

that she once rubbed cream

on until it healed.

PANDEMIC WITH THE POSSIBILITY OF DEATH

We will not be your body
bags, say the nurses
standing outside Mount
Sinai with photographs
of colleagues who've died.
She texts Lauren again,
Just give a thumbs up to
let me know you're okay
when you can. The nurses
are on her computer when
the prompt comes to get on
Zoom and join a chant.
Hi, Caitlin, calls Ramit
with her ex, Carla,
and a harmonium.
But they are not singing together.
Two voices, a few coughs
and a bark. *Please mute,*
types Sydra in the sidebar,
so that the rest of us can hear.
What does it mean to hear?
asked Carley's mom at which
point she said, *I have to go.*
There is something about to boil.
She clicks to leave the room
without a goodbye, opens other
portals. *My name is Leonardo,*

says her student whose email

says Leo. *I am in your Writing*

in the Workplace class at City

Tech. On Facebook, everyone

lists their jobs and things they hate.

I'm sorry the paper is late, says E.

I was in the hospital for two weeks

with symptoms and an underlying

condition. She is asked to package

her course in case she dies

by a woman named Erica.

She wakes in the night

Hi, Erica. I think I met you once

when there were no ink cartridges.

Your email gave me anxiety.

I don't want to lose income

or insurance,

but I can't do what you ask.

I'm sorry. Nobody can become

me after I am gone.

PANDEMIC WITH SLEEP

At night she dreams there
are three rooms open at once.
Like Zoom rooms. Only one
is sleep. She cannot close
the other rooms. One is
very prestigious. Empty oval
office edged with gold leaf.
Another is cruel. A taking
room of shame. Sleep is a purple
carpet from the 70's saying,
Fuck those others, come over
here. Didn't I tell you this
shit was coming? When America
was taken over by a cartoon
villain, we had to admit we
loved her, our beautiful
failed project on stolen
land. *I've been thinking of*
leaving for thirty-five years now,
said Lou Reed in "Blue
in the Face," *I'm almost ready.*
Strangers fucking on top of
parked cars, strangers stuck
underground walking in rows
up the stairs to see the light.
Strangers standing six feet apart.
It's been six days since she

asked her friend the nurse
at NYU Langone to let her
know she's okay. Of course
she isn't okay. Someone on
social media wonders if the
sirens are louder because
there is less other traffic.
Maybe so. She slices purple
garlic handed to her by the woman
smiling in a mask with a cartoon
smile at the farmers market, washed
in her lover's clean sink. Drops
it in the pan with the Irish butter
before frying the bright yellow eggs.
Oh New York we love you get up.

PANDEMIC WITH GRIEF AND LUNGS

In traditional Chinese medicine, *the lungs*
are connected with grief, writes
Po-Hong Yu, someone she doesn't know,
but who is breathing somewhere
on this earth, which we are grieving,
as this virus fills the lungs, as
the rain fills the rivers, the salt
cleanses the oceans the way
the eye rinses out soap with
tears. *I feel it in my chest,*
says her lover on a screen
about the grief of three people
over whose funerals she will soon
preside alone. Born with unformed
lungs, I couldn't filter the shared air
inside me; spent my first three weeks
in a machine. It's hard to breathe
with a mask; air rises and fogs
our glasses, making it hard to see.
We are tender in this grieving,
sent to our rooms to think
about what we've done
to the earth, to the animals,
to one another. Pema looked
peaceful on the screen, saying
the enlightened know that we
are born and die alone. Breathe

into that truth and know
that it true for each of us,
alone and together, falling
and rising on this tender earth.

PANDEMIC WITH REPRIEVE AND EMILY

And then there is a lull
in the sirens. A softness
to the morning, she
can hear actual birds,
no cars on the parkway,
a blessed reprieve.
She finds the phone
near the bed, types
birds to her friend who
is grieving, feeling the
weight of the world.
Closes her eyes again
and lets the gentleness
take her. Wakes again
to see her phone. *I've
been listening with my
eyes closed for half
an hour,* she said,
not one ambulance.
Her daughter sleeps
late, comes in for hugs.
They'll come later
in the day, but we'll
take it, this lull, safe
in our homes, a stove
that cooks, and candles
that light. Tonight, a full,

pink moon, as the red sea
split to allow passage.
I'm ceded, wrote
E.D., *I've stopped*
being Theirs. The
city of San Francisco
is so dark, the Milky
Way is visible over
the Golden Gate.
Not just now,
but always, each hand
we touch, or door
we pass through
is a privilege, plants
a seed. *Tell me about*
your liberation,
Gabe said, pouring
red wine, *this time*
consciously, of Grace—

PANDEMIC WITH NIGHTMARES

Red wine and salt—
unleavened papadums.
A scavenger hunt made by
the daughter to find the piece
of matzoh smuggled
from her lover's house.
Here is your first clue:
Go to something new
and blue. A bag that's use
was killed when a guy
ate a bat. Who Needs
Poetry. She wins
a coupon book. Free
hugs and "I'll clean
something." Dancing
to Darondo in the living
room: *Let My People Go.*
She falls asleep peaceful
and safe, but wakes to
her own inner sirens.
A dream of men
who think her house
is theirs; stand out
side her daughter/
little sister's room,
so that she must push
their slight white

bodies out the door

knowing the one

who looks like Dylann

Roof or Stephen

Miller will be back

like a battery that leaks

mercury. Her father

neglected to fully close

the door. By the time

he's back, she rallies

the whole family—

everyone inside, to press

with all their weight

against it, he's back,

pushing on the door

with such a force

that his hands are visible

through the wood,

like that toy, the *pinscreen*

you can press your face

against, and then his mouth,

his tongue. But the dream

spreads out; there are others

inside to tell the story too,

to build a new inside life

with, to help understand why

they must be vigilant as

they put away brown

bags of food,

that together, they

need to work together

to keep him out.

PANDEMIC WITH DISCO LIGHTS

When her lover is naked,
she is hers. When she is in
a black shirt and jeans,
she is coming toward her.
When she is in a suit
or religious garb, she
is someone who doesn't
know her, even if she
is eating a chocolate croissant
at her table on the morning
before Passover when she
is getting ready to bury
a body over Zoom. Tonight
the daughter went to her
Dad's and she mixed
a Q Tonic with Hendrick's,
some lime and lavender
bitters. Mustard with big
seeds. Chocolate and berries.
She talks to her friends
over video about porn.
I never go deep in there,
she tells them. *By the time*
I'm looking at porn, I'm
so close that all I need
is the little window of
a woman getting fucked

from behind on repeat
and I'm good to go. After
catching up on her shows,
and at seven, opening her window
to the courtyard, where
the luxury building dwellers
are on their decks, American
flag draped inside the rainbow one,
her neighbors in the old building
next door, everyone cheering
and banging old pans, she feels
it in her throat. Maybe David Lynch
is right. Maybe they'll come out
of this a better nation,
softer, more able to see one
another. Christine texts
from Corning that she's dancing
to DJ Nice. She puts on
her daughter's disco lights,
dances tiredly in the mirror,
swinging her arms with
three-pound weights to keep
the bones alive. Before sleep,
she makes her lover come
over the phone. *I'm deep inside you,*
she whispers from across Brooklyn,
as her lover moans softly,
trying not to wake the children.

PANDEMIC WITH PARTIAL RESURRECTION

The night before the resurrection,

she is too tired and tipsy

on wine and chocolate to hide

eggs, passes out next

to the daughter promising

to resurrect in the morning.

But sugar runs amok in her

blood like a terrorist,

like the sirens running

through the veins

of the sick city. At seven,

she hides eggs,

pastel marshmallow

and shimmery Cadbury,

behind books, perched on

paintings. Another scavenger

hunt: *She is taking the mask thing*

too far; radical tenderness;

the bookshelf with two sides.

Her friend texts: *The Easter*

Bunny is a sneaky bitch.

I can't take this anymore.

I need to see you.

I need to hug you. She wonders

if she could drive to Manhattan,

get her in the red car

whose windows won't open,

take her somewhere
like the wildlife refuge
her neighbor posted,
a road on a spit of land
in Jamaica Bay, stretching out
to a sky without ambulances.
But they can't touch.
She bikes by the Coney
Island hospital, rainbow
balloons adorn the gate
at the entrance as a stretcher
is carried inside. *You're
really going in?* asks
the barefooted Russian
man with a crackly smile
and no mask. The salt
water returns her
to herself, sort of. Body
tired of holding still,
holding grief, yellow bruise
on her right shoulder
from the weight of
another's head. Who
is used to holding
up the world?

PANDEMIC WITH SALT AND ANNIVERSARY

She drives to Rugby Road
where a woman has arranged
large sacks of root vegetables, swings
two in her trunk. They smile behind
masks. *Stay safe.* Drives to Carroll,
texts a woman named Molly, who
waves from inside as she leaves
her vegetables on her stoop. Twenty-
nine years ago today, in Ireland, she
was strapped to a hospital bed,
after telling the nurses if she
wasn't pregnant, she was fucking
being born. She spat in a man's
face as he strapped her down.
Today, she wakes thinking of
how her lover's mother used
to strap her down to remove
body hair, sculpt and tear her
into something other than
what the salt of her body
asked. *Feel your vertebrae drop
down to the earth like salt
in water,* says Genny Kapular
in her living room in Soho
zoomed into her living
room on Ocean Parkway
where she sits on her floor

while her lover sleeps,
letting her human body
be a human body. She roasts
the vegetables in oil and salt,
some sumac and cumin, will
feed them to her lover with
goat cheese, spinach, and eggs,
from the Aldefer Farm, and
her lover will wash her dishes
by hand, and make her bed,
with Guinevere the bear sitting
royally between pillows, her
Girls Be Poetic & Dirty T-shirt
folded lovingly on top.
Maybe she was being born,
afterward, like after this,
she would never be the same.

PANDEMIC WITH BIRTHDAY

The sun is shining this morning,
and when we woke from
the nightmares, we were gentle
with ourselves. We held ourselves.
Didn't worry too much about
meaning, or language, let the
body be a body making stories
in the ether, let sleep be something
worth surrendering to.
So the body feels okay
this morning, salt settling
in the ocean, half a century
here on this planet that loves
us enough to let us go.
Today, April 16, is Aimee's
birthday. We were supposed
to have a disco party at her house
in the woods in Woodstock,
which is a work of art. Antiques
repurposed, golds and teal
and earthy reds. Kinetic
black and white art. Merce
Cunningham. The Buddha
sitting, saying *Shhhh*. A blown-
up picture of her son's toes
after he had painted them
with *aaallll* the polish. Instead,

we will be together apart on
screens, which are an illusion,
as much as distance is. This
poem is for Aimee, whose
name means *love*, who is
a dancer and can dance
through the darkest places
in us and help us move
toward light. Aimee has a
birthmark on her breast;
she loves spicy food, red
wine, she'll talk to me in my
car when I don't know
where to go, when shame
is a red flower blooming
that she's not afraid to touch,
let stand in the vase. Her face,
I miss her face. At Bard,
she had a nose ring,
so when I was in the hospital
in Galway on April 15, 1991,
the only nurse I trusted
had a nose ring. She quit,
but never mind. Aimee makes
me laugh after I'm done
crying, which she doesn't
ask me to stop. We used
to run naked to the library
in the rain, in the wee
hours of the morning,

after fighting about
stories in our hearts. Aimee
is an Aries, and fiery, her
flavors are raspberry,
chocolate, and cayenne.
We cook sweet potatoes and
thick leafy greens, adding
raisins, because fuck it,
there is no reason to separate
the sweet from spice.

PANDEMIC WITH TRANSITION

At night, they put on gold eyeshadow
and wigs to be new on Zoom
where they dance to music
from living rooms in Los Angeles
to Florida, to Seattle, to what looks
like the moon. The effort
leaving them a little sad
and too tired to even make it
through the rose and thorn.
My thorn is that you got mad
about gargling the salt water
to bring down the swelling
in your mouth because the dentists
are closed. She wakes
remembering the tent
and sleeping bags left
in her ex's car. Breathing
should be easier, open
the trunk, the lungs,
let it out, there is only
so much air. Sleeps again,
until the daughter comes in
from a dream of a tsunami
at a beach with her class
and all the parents. *You*
couldn't find your car, she
says, resting her whole body

on her right shoulder,
so we got in with someone else,
then watched it get caught
up in the waves, little red
car with mixed-up fuses
swimming away. In the morning,
one mom sends a picture from
the school fundraiser five years
prior, *Sip into Spring,* all the women
in dresses with rosé wine,
huddled for a selfie. *Will*
life ever look like that again?
she writes, beaming shoulder
to shoulder, though she
remembers feeling like
she was trying hard to
smile at the time. *Maybe*
you should go to work, says
the governor to the sitting
president on TV. *Maybe*
you should not call April
a month, says Taylor
Mac, on Instagram,
but a transition.

PANDEMIC WITH SOCIAL DISTANCE
AND ZOMBIES

They meet in the park
five weeks after they shared
flourless chocolate cake
at Hamilton's, both forks
stopping before they met
in the middle, the night
before the restaurants closed,
before the germ circles
shrank. They stand six
feet apart, keep the daughters
six feet apart, so they hug
one another through trees.
Masks keeping out the
thickest pollen ever recorded.
Why does love sometimes
feel so much like saying
we're sorry? The dreams
are worse after red
wine, she's discovered,
when the virus becomes
a male intruder she must
remove, a storm of seas
for her daughter, a slow
dance with a stranger
for her friend across town.
Handshakes were overrated

anyway, they agree. Why touch
if you can't embrace, why
the petri dish without the
pleasure. Aimee writes
of looking out her window
at wildly blooming forsythia
as a seventy-eight-year-old woman
with the virus tells her
the thing that she's sick
of is her kids telling her
what to do. An image
of protestors in Ohio
crowding their governor's office,
angry about closures
looks like a zombie
horror still. MAGA hats,
a joker's mask, a blonde
lady screaming. *Black studies
called white supremacy a death
cult for 35 years*, writes Kaitlyn
Greenidge on Twitter,
and pretty much predicted this image,
that also portrays why
we might never go
back to school, at least
not, like so many things,
in the way we once knew.

PANDEMIC WITH ELVIS IN THE BUILDING

This morning what I want to hold
onto is the dream about the horse.
We are, my daughter and I, touching
her wildness. Running our hands down
her ropey mane, the muscular jaw shiny
with golden brown, even her mouth
that licks our hands and snorts with
approval, or hunger, our fingers run
down her slick, strong back.
After touching the horse, we touch
the sword, bringing with it all the
power of that wildness and freedom.
The sword is wet with horsepower.
The sword is gleaming. Why do girls
draw horses? Cocks are not the muscular
thing they want to ride on. Cocks
can't take us anywhere new. On a
horse, you open your legs and ride
far way. Yesterday was too much
beauty. The lover pulled her chair
close to feel bodies touch, cumin
and coriander wafting up to high
ceilings. Campari and ginger
on the tongue. Lizzo on a screen. Green
trees out windows dancing in breeze,
singing *A Change is Gonna Come*.
But out on the street in the morning,

she must wait to be invited back in
after an important call, and a hole
forms in her chest. Like all times
she's been on the outside
of shut doors. On the beach,
they are alone under her cowboy hat,
as she describes the light of the blue
sky, light of her gold hair, gold
twine of the hat's brim. The ocean
forgives, again and again. But by
the end of the day, some new light
shines through and blinds her eyes.
She can't tell if she's crying
because the one they've chosen
to replace the racist in power
uses racism to fight him. Or
because they watched a show
about high school kids crouching
in corners when a gun goes off.
Or some bitter taste
in her mouth she can't name.
The kids say goodbye
with their phones, tell truths,
apologize and forgive, tell
one another what they mean.
She's crying on the couch, daughter
holding her hand. Maybe
it's because she was teaching
high school when this happened,
and Nikki asked her if she'd have

hidden them in lockers and stood
by the door to get shot like Vicki Soto;
her own daughter across town
in the arms of strangers. Or maybe
because we're living through something
like this now, hiding in rooms
so an intruder can't see us. Telling
the truth, telling one another
what we mean. Not knowing
which of us will come out alive.
Or maybe it's just the limits of love,
all the beauty that will end when
the world hops back on its blind
train. Its crowded hallways lined
with lockers, each holding what
few things we need, the lessons
they decided to teach, the stories
of who we thought we were. All run
by a greedy power we can't touch.
But by the doorway, between
the bars, a bright light shines
through, and on the other side,
waits a horse and a sword
and a map. And she'll kneel
on the dirt and hoist her daughter
up, kiss her soft cheek, tell her
to head toward the sun.

PANDEMIC WITH JEKYLL AND MOON

Today is Earth Day, the sun
is here, ready or not. The night
holds terrors as old as the moon,
which is new today. The wound
glows; the night, an ocean of dark.
The virus, the face of the man
who comes in the night,
at the bottom of night's black
bowl, becomes all faces,
becomes faceless. In order
to breathe in, we must exhale.
To love, we must face dying
alone. To come together,
we must stay apart. *Hold me,*
I asked as the sun peeked
through the shades and she
was still in dream. *Fold you?*
she asked, waking. Sigh. *New
beginnings are often disguised
as painful endings,* says the fake
quote from Lao Tzu. Fold me,
darling. Take the sides
of me, both black and white,
and let them touch, make
of me something that can
be carried. Fold me into
the moon's new light.

PANDEMIC WITH NETWORKS

Under the ground,
the mycelial web
connects thousand-
year trees whose bark
holds knowledge in touch,
like our skin, as we withhold
it, except in portals where
it pours out. On my screen
this morning, Ariana reads
Inanna, who traveled to heaven
and the underworld and back.
Her lips are the color of dark
plums, skin an impossible
gold, androgynous eyes
broken from truth and travel.
She's joined by readers
around the world on screens
through a network started
by a boy from whom
we'd turned away.
The loosening of the hair
The binding of the hair
For the new moon
in Taurus, Chani Nicholas
writes, *I know that our world*
is rearranged,
Right is wrong. Up

is down ... greed will always
propagate the myth
that there isn't enough.
Meanwhile, the virus
takes Elizabeth Warren's
big brother. *What made him*
extra special was his smile, she writes
online, *quick and crooked, it always*
seemed to generate its own light . . .
While this pandemic has
been happening, Trump *has signed*
an executive order
allowing mining on the moon
says Arundahti Roy.
We wake now when our bodies
wake, turn off the machines.
Cars stop except for those
with sirens. Trees scream
ultrasonically when thirsty
or in pain. I sleep through
the wail of the ambulances
some nights, others, it hits
the chord of dream that startles
the body back to waking,
like Inanna at the shore of Uruk
with truth and dagger, black
garment; garment of color,
ready to restore the city
and its children back
from the flood of betrayal.

PANDEMIC WITH ATMOSPHERE

When you say you want entrance
to poems, I feel fingers inside me.
Barometric shifts swell glands
in my neck, sending an aura
out around my skull. *Yes, me too,*
writes my friend in Harlem,
yesterday and today. Also, my lover's
son, awake in pain. More evidence of
interconnectedness, not just to one
another, but to the pull of the earth
and its salt, its seas. Here, in New York,
we are pitied by the rest of the country,
and in the rest of the country, by the world.
The belief that "freedom" is literally more important
than life, writes Fintan O'Toole in the Irish
Times, has *infused a very large part of American culture*,
has laid the groundwork for the death march
we watch from our windows, where I keep
leaving my wooden spoons and pans after
the 7 p.m. cheer. *No time for love like now,*
sings Michael Stipe from a screened porch,
on my little phone screen. He's always held
mortality in his burning board voice,
maybe why his songs became the anthems
for our friend Stephen, dying young
of another disease in the lungs, where grief
is held. Why roots underground are often

the image for breath. Supposedly,

the curve is flattened, but nobody knows

who's been touched or when hands

can meet; when we can listen to music

in parks on warm nights, looking up

at branches against indigo light,

lying together on their deep roots,

as the old earth breathes in

cello notes, sudden drums, the globe

of the skull nestled

in another body's lap.

PANDEMIC WITH NEWS CYCLE

She knows better than to check
the news before bed, but she does
it anyway. Loneliness. Habit, a need
for a hit. What she gets is a cut
to the heart, a tip to the balancing
act on the tripwire she's walking
to say things are okay. Lorna Breen
was her name. The headline reads
Top E.R. Doctor who Treated Virus
Patients Dies by Suicide. A photo
of a woman with a broad smile,
one year younger than we are
all turning this year on Zoom.
She tried to do her job and it killed her,
said her father. She'd told him
about an onslaught of patients
dying before they could be taken
out of the ambulances. Wouldn't
stop showing up at work even
when she was directed to rest,
to recover from the virus herself.
We need to do more than clap
for these people, says someone
on Facebook. But what can
we do beyond virtual outcry
and banging out windows,
bicker about the canceled primary,

wear masks with the word *VOTE*
over our mouths. Eavan Boland died
yesterday, also, in Ireland, age seventy-five,
of a stroke. *There is no place here*
for the inexact praise of the easy
graces and sensuality of the body,
she wrote in a poem titled
"Quarantine," in 2008. *There is only*
time for this merciless inventory.
Did you hear about the Oxford vaccine
and the monkeys? texts her lover
as she's getting ready for sleep,
head now too heavy for her
frame. *I didn't hear about*
the monkeys, she types, waits
for the three dots, shifts to sleep
mode where she'll dream
of hotel swimming pools,
Christmas trees, all the
ways we used to huddle
together in easy grace
and gratitude. Thank you,
Lorna Breen, for your service.
No pots or pans or Blue Angels
overhead can bring you back,
but we'll say your name.

PANDEMIC WITH OLIVES AND MUSIC

The headline reads: *Trump rapidly*
uses wartime power for meat, hesitates
for ventilators. The headline reads:
Beloved Brooklyn teacher, 30, dies
of coronavirus after she was twice
denied testing. She died not only
because of COVID-19, but because
we live in a world that is racist
and anti-black, says a dear friend
of Rana Zoe Mungin. She taught
at a school near one where I once
taught, had an MFA, we had two
mutual queer friends. Meanwhile, Pence
doesn't wear a mask. The president
doesn't wear a mask. I can smell pussy
inside my mask biking home from
my lover, who I'm scared will stop
seeing me when she tells her ex-wife
that her germ circle's been made larger
than she knew. She made me an Aperol
spritz to go, bitter orange on my tongue.
My therapist wants to start by asking
how it feels to be drinking alcohol
during our session. *It's not nearly as big*
a deal as the fact that we are on fucking
screens, I tell her. *I want you to do*
something that's not on a screen, I tell

my daughter, in a pile on her bed
for hours, sometimes chuckling deeply
in a way that both softens me
and makes me wonder when she'll share
the company of other kids. *Okay, I'll dye
my hair purple*, she answers, and does.
Making dinner, after the 7 p.m. window cheer,
I leave it open to hear my neighbors
play *Empire State of Mind*, text friends
in California to ask them if they think
I can eat the olives that sat in my car
for five days after the farmer's market.
Eight million stories out there in the Naked City,
sings Jay-Z, *It's a pity half of y'all won't make it.*
Probs just fine, texts Forest Moon, *considering
how ancient Greeks kept their olives in giant pottery
in the heat for months.* At the end of the night
I turn on the disco lights, try to make K.
dance to *This Year* by The Mountain Goats,
but she just lies on the couch, offering me
her feet with which to sway. Close
the windows. It's beginning to rain.
I'm gonna make it through this year,
if it kills me, sing the Goats.
Turn out the colored lights.
Time for sleep, after the dance,
after the warm salt water
gargle for that one
tender tooth.

PANDEMIC WITH CITY AND ENDINGS

And then she drove out of the city.

Past road-signs flashing *STAY AT HOME*,

past empty malls and closed down superstores

'til the interstate was flanked with trees and skies,

country houses with homemade yard-signs

thanking essential workers with rainbows and hearts,

for a night on a lake in the woods. The only sounds

a blue heron, a trout splashing, bumble bee caught

on the screen porch. *How do you want to live out*

the end of the world? Your own and all of ours?

Her Baruch student, sends a recording

of his voice telling her about lighting a spark

inside himself to become a fire that spreads.

Ula, the woman at the cottage next door,

apologizes for not wearing a mask as she helps

turn the boat back on its belly on the dock

before her drive home. The Mobil station

offers free gloves for pumping gas. She drives

fast, as she's late to retrieve the daughter

from her father. They've walked to her house

and back to wait. *Outside Without a Mask?*

the sign says entering Brooklyn,

How Sweet It Is! They'll drive again, later,

she and the daughter, to catch the sunset

behind Coney Island, the Ferris Wheel halted mid-

circle, like a wind-up toy with no one to crank

the key. She'll fall asleep holding her,

and wake to her back with a bad dream
about bees, head burrowed in her shoulder's
crevice. Morning mercifully offers some hours
before the sirens start. Her neighbor writes
the whole building to say she's acquired
an oximeter if anyone needs;
here is her phone, the number
on her door. We will live
out the end much the way
we lived out the middle,
but the bread will smell stronger,
the pink of the tulips brighter, breath
of the child next to us
softer in our ears.

PANDEMIC WITH FLIES AND LIES

I wake to texts from N.:
I have cancer. Trump has Covid
and I have cancer. I am speaking,
Kamala says firmly, when
Pence tries to interrupt her
from behind his Plexiglas
with a fly stuck to his head.
The school across the street
is closed because the Hasidic
community in Borough Park
refuses to wear masks, torches
them in piles, shutting down
traffic for their dying idols,
their last gasp. I drive to the
Bronx for a Pap Smear and
a man coughs on me on the
street. *There is opportunity*
in crisis, says Maya Wiley
on the radio. What if we'd
refused, writes M.G., to ask
for less...? Empty office
buildings glowing like bee
hives or Anne Hamilton
exhibits. Art on wood
panels covering shuttered
shops. At home, scrolling
between articles about death

rates and doom, she clicks
on an ad for a pink pan with
a 30,000 person waitlist.
It is elegant, breast-like,
from the past or future.
32,867 people have died
of COVID in NYC. What
can that pan do? Today,
the president will address
the nation from his balcony
like cartoons of kings as
people gather to die
on the south lawn. *You're*
caught up for now, says
her phone screen, at the
end of the news scroll.
Are you called anything
other than Caitlin, texts
the new lover, who brings
her flowers, slowly
tells the story behind
her scars, sends a letter
from the future about
repair for the pan sized
hole in her heart. People
are no longer clapping
from balconies. They
are taking to the streets,
protesting on the red steps
of times square, biking

from Columbus Circle,

on Indigenous Peoples Day

marching over bridges

chanting *Say Her Name.*

Facebook tells her four

years ago, she dreamed

of holding a door shut

against a president who

could come through walls.

mama, meowma, child,

caitie, ms.grace. the goat.

Breonna Taylor, Breonna Taylor

Breonna Taylor. Twenty-six days.

Winter is coming

They are putting things

in jars. One door

will shut. Keep watching

the open windows.

PANDEMIC WITH COUNTING AND MIDDLE

There was no landslide,
Not even a rooftop
from which to yell.
There was a courtyard, a walk
by the river with an ex,
a bench where they toasted
with decent red wine in
plastic cups, shared
their latest failures in love.
The house on the lake
was packed for the winter;
boats on their bellies,
Zoe's applewood stacked
by the fireplace, jar
of letters jammed
without words. The latest
lover wouldn't be coming
anymore, but the autumn
paper flowers tied in a rose
bow stayed remarkably alive.
Middle sister, was she doomed
to be a place in-between?
The High Line Hotel TV
screen was split between
red & blue. For three nights,
she woke every two hours
to check the count. *Professor,*

you look tired, says her student

on zoom. Just a voice and

a name and a square. *I*

look like a tiger? she asked.

audio muffled over wires,

drowned by construction below.

There was no repudiation, no

correction of where they'd gone

off course. She looks to see

if repudiation is the right word,

and loses thirty minutes in her

phone. Fingers itchy with trauma,

It looks as though they will take Philly,

now, and Georgia, too. At night,

before bed, the daughter finds

something smelly in her bag.

It is not food. It is death or

waste; she makes the daughter

sit next to her as she reaches

in with the towel. Makes her

swear its not a prank or

anything she knows, just

another aberration of this year,

which has them sitting

on the kitchen floor, laughing

and crying at the stench.

When the daughter comes in

her bed in the night,

she is dreaming of a car

that can leave America

to a place with hills,

and stone houses.

Wild animals and people

outside, working together

without masks. In the middle

of the village is a building,

and in the middle

of the building is a pool.

On one side of the pool

is a body floating. Death

and debris circling out.

On the other side, children

splash and play. A woman

puts her hand on her shoulder,

says they need her help.

They need to clear the pool.

They need to be brave enough

to get near the body.

They need to clean it out.

PANDEMIC WITH GRATEFUL AND GASLIGHTS

The trees are damp and bare
They have given it their all;
will now hold one another
up, waiting for winter. Inside,
there is a fire. The flames
flare up with a mask-less
mouth's low blow. Art is dead,
the man, my stepfather, not the infinite
wish to hold the world still.
A transition of power will happen,
even as 45 denies and collects.
In the 1944 film, the husband dims
the flames of gas; denies
the darkening world.
What does it mean to call harm
imaginary? To call dark light?
The first thing you tell me
about your past
maps our story; mothers
and fathers crowding in or
turning away map the way
we look for love. *Did you know*
I became a woman? my daughter
asks my mother from the back-
seat on speakerphone in the red car
as we drive through the dark
on the day that marks the day we

pretend we are celebrating
something consensual.
Call it gratitude. Call it giving.
Glad to be reminded of another
passage, my mother tells me to hand
the phone to my daughter, voices
together over wires, as I blink and
steady my wandering eyes
at the oncoming brights
on this long night's
twisting roads.

PANDEMIC WITH AFTER

After a night when I dug
into the flesh on my thigh
to remove what I thought
was a tick, but wasn't, I am
ready to be gentle. I am ready
to put my hand on the head
of the feral animal barking
with fear and protection
inside my chest. After
we have lost almost
everything, doors shut
on love that hurts, is
rationed, not enough. After
a night of deep, drugged sleep,
animals burrowed in the walls,
glass shattered in dreams. After
she's left the pink leather tie
on a pillow in a hammock to be
retrieved by her ex and replaced
by something red and strappy.
After the second wave and winter
when we weigh ourselves
with blankets filled with glass,
text our friends when we want
to crawl into a ditch. Then, finally,
after this is over, what will come next?
If we are going to come out of this

crisis less selfish than when we went in,
writes Pope Francis, *we need*
to let ourselves be touched
by other's pain. In bed this morning,
I text Zoe and Nicole the place
on my thigh where I went digging
for something imaginary burrowed.
N. says she will spare us the image
of her new three-inch scar where
yesterday, they removed the last
of the cancerous nodes. Instead,
she sends us a picture of her
young and smoking in her bra.
You see me, she texts. After
this is over, I want to stretch
out. I want my worth. I want
to be worthy. I want to reach
and hold you, teach and learn
you, love that opens
windows, integrity,
lungs that empty, mouths
that bare. I want time
to heal. I want to feel
like a whole animal,
not a sum of parts.
I want to see you.
I want to be seen.

ACKNOWLEDGEMENTS

Thankful to all of these people and/or organizations who are quoted or referred to in these pages, or have otherwise helped me get through whether you know it or not. Thank you, thank you, for saving me over and over in a myriad of ways:

Aimee Gallin, Alissa Quart, Allison Warren, Amani King, Amy Newton, Amy Shearn, Anna McKewan, Anne Hamilton, Anne Haven McDonnell, Anthony Cappo, Ariana Reines, Ariel Friedman, Arundahti Roy, Ashley Sanders, Betsy Andrews, Breonna Taylor, Bruce Barrett, Callen-Lorde Community Health Clinic, Carla Roitz, Carla Strangenberg, Carley Moore, Cathy James, Chani Nicholas, Cheryl Clarke, Chris Wells, Christine Atkins, Clarence Major, Dari Litchman, Darondo, David Victor Rose, Deborah Copaken, Della, DJ Nice, Domenick Ammirati, Eavon Boland, Elizabeth Scarboro, Elizabeth Warren, Elka Gotfryd, Emily Cass McDonnell, Emily Dickinson, Evalena Leedy, Eve Pearlman, Fintan O'Toole, Forest Moon Melchior, Frances Coles Burroughs, Gabriel Metcalf, Genny Kapular, Gina Magid, Hamilton's, Hope Moriki, Jay-Z, Jennifer Taub, Jeremiah Fox, Joaquin Baca-Asay, John Prine, Joseph Legaspi, Joshua Kurtz, Julie Pepito, Kaitlin Greenridge, Kamala Harris, Karen Zuckerberg, Karyn Kloumann, Kate Femoile, Kate Sergel Buncher, Kathleen McDonnell, Kaya Hope Friedman, Kevin Morby, Kiese Layman, Ladd Spiegel, Lao-Tzu, Lauren Kollar, Leonard Cohen, Leonardo Collado, Leslie Unruh, Lizzo, Lorna Breen, Lou Reed, Madeline Cass-Estin, Malka Longabucco,

Masha Gessen, Matt Longabucco, Maya Wiley, Merav Ben Horin, Michael Stipe, Michelle and Barack Obama, Millie Bobby Brown, Naomi Extra, Neighborhood Coop Food Project, Nicole Callihan, Octavia Butler, Pamela Adlon, Patti Smith, Pema Chodren, PJ Harvey, Po-Hong-Yu, Pope Francis, Queen, Rachel Swersey, Rachel Timoner, Ramit Kreitner, Rana Zoe Mungin, Rebecca Solnit, Renata Segura, Safia Jama, Sarah Hansen, Sasha Slocombe, Secret City, Shana Hamilton, Sherine Gilmour, Suzan Alparslan, Sydra Mallery, Tara Pontani, the Mobil station on Coney Island Ave, the Park Slope Food Coop, the Putnam Market, Vicki Soto, Victor LaValle, Vivian Yamato, Yolander Soler, Zoe Ryder White

ABOUT THE AUTHOR

Caitlin Grace McDonnell was a New York Times Poetry Fellow at NYU where she received her MFA. She has published a chapbook, *Dreaming the Tree* (belladonna books 2003) and a book, *Looking for Small Animals* (Nauset Press 2012). She teaches writing in Brooklyn, NY, and lives with her daughter, Kaya Hope.

A note on a type symbol used throughout the book:

✳

The image was discovered in a font called *1698 Almanach Symbols* by GLC. The font is inspired by printers' disintegrating and tired fonts from the sixteenth century to the early twentieth century. In 1698, an outbreak of the second plague pandemic hit Europe. This eroded asterisk embodies an abstraction of how the COVID-19 virus particle looks, suitable for a cycle of poems about a pandemic, especially since it may have been used as a printer's mark during a previous pandemic.

GLC — Gilles Le Corre
La Grande Fonsonnière
Talmont Saint Hilaire, 85440
France

Mrs. Eaves is the body type, and *Wicked Grit* is used for the poem titles.